NO WEAPON FORMED

21 Days Of Inspiration

SABRINA BOONE

Copyright © 2020 Sabrina Boone

All rights reserved. No portion of this book may be reproduced in any form without permission from the publisher, except as permitted by U.S. copyright law. For permissions request write to the publisher addressed "Attention Permission Coordinator"

authorsabrinanboone@gmail.com

ISBN: 978-0-578-65877-3

Ordering Information: *For information about special discounts available for bulk purchases, sales promotions, fund-raising and educational needs, contact above email.*

Dedication

First and foremost I'd like to thank **God** for giving me the vision and pushing me. **Lord** you have really shown me that I can do ALL things through **Christ** who strengthens me!

To my three children you guys are my heartbeats; **Aunye, Zahmir** and **Zanaa.**

Thank you to my parents **Frank** and **Pam** and my stepmother **Wendy**, you guys support everything that I do and I appreciate it. Thank you to **Larry** for being an awesome father and taking on full responsibility when I needed to study or meditate, even when I just needed peace and quiet to think you stepped right in and took care of the children!

Thank you to **Odessa G. White** for believing in my vision and being the most passionate, realest, professional publisher a girl could have!

Thank you to my Prophetic Mentor for always having my back and keeping it 100 at all times; **Prophet David Artis** and my **Sniper Nation Family**. Thank you to my **True Love Church family,** and Spiritual Parents **Apostles Owen** and **Julia Ford**, thank you for always having my back and being there when I need you. Thank you to all who played a part in this project which is way too many to name just know that you're in my heart!

Acceleration, Elevation, and Double Portion = Now is the time let's do this!!
Love you all to life, Sabrina!

Day 1

I can do all things through Christ who strengthens me.

--Philippians 4:13 KJV

Yes you can...

This is one of my favorite scriptures. It's very powerful, we need to apply it to our lives daily. Often times we read and recite scriptures but do we apply them to our daily lives? Do we even comprehend what we're reading? The scripture says we can do ALL things through Christ who strengthens us, so why do we speak failure into our lives?

Many times we encourage others but we don't encourage ourselves. We have to believe that God will do all things. We have to have faith and learn to trust that God will give us the strength and endurance we need to press forth and be strong. If we fight, God will fight for us and with us! God gives us what we need and not what we want..

Father, I pray that you remove the I don't know how, the can't do ,and I'm not good enough thoughts out of our minds and replace them with I can and I will. Father lead us, guide us and help us to decree and declare strength, In Jesus name...

Amen

Day 2

KINGDOM BUILDING

For a time is coming when people will no longer listen to sound and wholesome teaching. They will follow their own desires and will look for teachers who will tell them whatever their itching ears want to hear. They will reject the truth and chase after myths.

--2 Timothy 4:3-4

We have so many people spreading God's word but putting a remix on it to appease themselves. They claim to want to win souls for the Kingdom, but instead they add and subtract from the word of God to satisfy their own flesh. Here's an example: You've been reaching out and talking to a brother or sister in Christ, they invite you out for "fellowship" at a restaurant. You both order food, You began to notice that they've had multiple glasses of wine, so you question their actions, so they began to explain by telling you that the bible says in 1Timothy 5:23 DRINK NO LONGER WATER, BUT USE A LITTLE WINE FOR THY STOMACH'S SAKE AND THINE OFTEN INFIRMITIES. So now you're all confused, but in all actuality the scripture doesn't mean that at all. Paul was drinking grape juice, the water could have been bad or he may have simply mixed the juice with water.

We can pour misleading information into someone else and they won't be able to decipher the truth. This is what happens when we don't study the content of scriptures and use them for our own personal gain. We have to be mindful of what we let people pour into us.

Father, I pray that you open our ear gates to hear your voice and only your voice. Give us discernment to know right from wrong. Keep our hearts and minds covered so that we will always be in the spirit and not the flesh., Lord you are the way, the truth, and the life. In Jesus name...

Amen

Day 3

REMAIN HUMBLE

Do not be quick with your mouth, do not be hasty in your heart to utter anything before God. God is in heaven and you are on earth, so let your words be few.

--Ecclesiastes 5:2

Sometimes we pray, pray, pray, and pray some more, but we don't give God the glory that he deserves. Some people only pray for their selfish needs, like a new job, house, car, money etc. That's fine but what about being persistent, God already knows what we are in need of. Do we take the time to thank Him for all He has already done? Do we tell him how much we adore Him, how much we love Him, how grateful we are for all the blessings we have received already. We don't need to give God a long list of our needs and wants. Sometimes a thank you Lord is all He needs to hear.

Father, we pray that our prayers become more persistent and that we continue to give you praise, honor and glory.
In Jesus name...
Amen

Day 4

THE BATTLE IS NOT YOURS

The lord will fight for you; you need only be still.

--Exodus 14:14

Sometimes we get ourselves into situations and we go to everyone else for help but God. God has all the answers to everything that we need. God already knows what the outcome will be. Will we trust Him? Will we believe that He can work it out? Will we let Him do the fighting for us? We get in the way of ourselves! There's nothing that God can't handle. This is where our faith comes into play, we panic and ask for all the wrong help. All we have to do is ask God for help and ask Him to lead our paths or ask what it is that we need to do. We have to learn how to sit still and listen to God. We will lose every battle trying to do things without the help of God. *Father, I pray that we will be led to you at all times. I pray that in our times of weakness that we seek you, and trust in your power and glory. Allow us to be still and just let you work. In Jesus name…*
Amen.

Day 5

GOOD DEEDS

Do nothing out of selfish ambition or vain conceit. Rather, in humility value others above yourselves.

--Phillipians 2:3

Often times we start off doing a good deed for someone, but then pride can kick in. Let's just say someone forgot their lunch money so you offer to buy them lunch. Did you do it because you really cared about them or did you do it for selfish reasons? A person that shows humility would just buy the lunch and keep it moving and expect nothing back in return. A vain person would spread the word around to everyone how they had to buy you lunch, or constantly remind you of it every time they see you, making you feel as if you owe them something. The Bible says *"But when you give to the needy, do not let your left hand know what the right is doing, so that your giving may be in secret. And your Father who sees in secret will reward you."*

Father, we thank you for keeping us humble, gentle, and kind. Thank you for allowing us to be your servants and serving others so that we can get your glory.

In Jesus name…

Amen

Day 6

FATHER CAN YOU HEAR ME

If my people who were called by my name, will humble themselves and pray and seek my face and turn from their wicked ways, then I will hear from heaven, and I will forgive their sins and will heal their lands.

--2Chronicle 7:14

We may go through so many things and we tend to not remember God. We'll call on everyone else to fix our problems instead of calling on God himself. We start to blame everyone else for all the things that are happening in our lives, but in all honesty we need to take a deeper look at ourselves. We need to begin to have a real conversation with God and repent.

Be honest, tell God how much you need Him, and how much you love Him. Ask God to guide you and help lead you. When you go to God you must go wholeheartedly. Change your mindsets and once God sees that you are serious and honest, He will begin to answer your prayers. He will forgive and fix your old mindset.

Father, I pray that you fix us Lord, change our mindsets, change our walk, change our talk. Lead us Lord, so that we can lead others into salvation. I pray that we keep seeking you and only you and that we repent so that we can be forgiven so that we will get the glory of your healing.

In Jesus name...

Amen

Day 7

LISTEN

Understand this my dear brothers and sisters: You must be quick to listen, slow to speak, and slow to get angry.

--James 1:19

If you're walking around mean and angry, do you really think that God is pleased with you? Do you totally trust God to give you a clear mindset, and the proper words to say before you speak or get angry? Do you take the time to listen to what's going on around you before you react? When God is in control of your life you'll begin to take the time to listen because He will give you the patience to do so. It's when God is not in control that our minds wander and we fail to take the time to think and talk straight. This is when you start to blurt out a bunch of words which have no meaning. Don't get me wrong sometimes we all have natural reactions, but we must also have discipline and obedience.

Father, you are always in control of our actions, our minds, and our tongues. Lord convict our heart, mind, and spirit if you hear us talking unlike you. We only want to use our voices for your glory.

In Jesus name...

Amen

Day 8

KEEP PRESSING

Let us not become weary in doing good, for at the proper time we will reap a harvest if we do not give up.

> --Galatians 6:9

We all can grow weary thinking that we have done all that we could and that God just doesn't hear us sometimes. Keep pushing because at the right time which is God's timing all the things that you've prayed for will come to fruition. We have to be patient! We have to stay still! We have to pray without ceasing and stay saturated in His word.

If God tells you to do something you need to be obedient and do it. Things don't happen overnight but it will happen. The word says you should be good to all men, especially those in the household of faith.

Father, we thank you in advance for all that you have blessed us with and the blessings that are to come. Lord continue to help us stay flat foot and planted in your word. Lord I pray that we all offer unto you a perfect sacrifice.

In Jesus name...

Amen

Day 9

TIME TO SUIT UP

Put on all of God's armor so that you will be able to stand firm against all strategies of the devil.

--Ephesians 6:11

The devil will try to attack you in so many different ways. You have to remain strong and know how to fight back. If you show weakness he will continue to get over on you, but if you use the tools that God has given you; you will always conquer him.

The word says resist the devil and he will flee. We fight with The word of God, prayer, righteousness, salvation, faith, truth, and the Spirit. As long as we keep all these things we will always defeat the devil.

Father, we pray that you will always cover us and protect us from anything that's not of you, keep us in our full armor at all times.

In Jesus name...

Amen

Day 10

LET YOUR LIGHT SHINE

Jesus answered, "I am the way and the truth and the life. No one comes to the Father except through me".

--John 14:6

Many people like to use this scripture when evangelizing. People often ask how could you believe in a God that you can't see? Jesus told Philip, *"don't you know me, Philip, even after I have been among you for such a long time? Anyone who has seen me has seen the Father."* You don't have to see God to know that He is real! You have to believe in Jesus, and believe in His word, and believe that He is the path to heaven. The only way into heaven is through His Son. Jesus died for our sins and rose from the dead so that we could have a new life. It is our job to tell others about sin, righteousness, and about judgement. So that we can all get into heaven with God.

Father, I pray that you let our lights shine forever and they will not go dim.
In Jesus name...
Amen

Day 11

HE HEARS US

And if we know that he hears us, whatever we ask we know that we have what we asked of him.

--1John 5:15

We all need to pray that God hears us whenever we talk to Him. We should pray for ourselves and for others. We should also pray about things that have happened in our lives and things that we have done to others. We should ask for forgiveness from the things we have done, said, or thought that wasn't of God. We have to have faith and know that God will do all that we ask of Him as long as it's according to His will. Sometimes we have to endure hardships to accomplish His purpose for us. We have to endure but keep believing. We have to know that our prayers will be answered.

Father, I pray that everyone forms an open and honest line of communication with you through prayer and may you clear their ears to hear only your voice and direction.

In Jesus name...

Amen

Day 12

ONLY GOD

So let it grow, for when your endurance is fully developed you will be perfect and complete, needing nothing.

--James 1:4

There will be hard times and there will be easy times, but having a mixture of the good and bad helps our faith in God grow. In the midst of everything that happens we have to trust God. Trusting God with all your heart is what makes us grow stronger. If things were good all the time we wouldn't have anything to test our faith. It's when we continuously trust God and believe in His word that we build up our faith. It's all about having a relationship with God; our Father. We gain endurance with each situation that we go through. It's ok to start over, we may fall down but God will pull us back up. Going through difficult times is a stepping stool for growth.

Train yourselves to stand firm and not be moved. Prayer, reading the Bible, meditating on the word, fasting, laying still, and listening for God's directions is all that we need. God will never leave us or forsake us. You have to do the work and seek God and trust that our Father will make you complete and you won't be in need of nothing but Him.

Father, I ask that you keep us in your presence. Continue to lead and guide us, continue to walk with us. Give us the strength to follow your lead and not be led astray.

In Jesus name…

Amen

Day 13

KEEP THE FAITH

I have fought the good fight, I have finished my course, I have kept the faith

--2 Timothy 4:7

Paul gave this charge to Timothy right before his death, He gave him three positive statements about his ministry. *(First)* Paul gave Timothy confidence to fight the good fight of faith; meaning we have to fight against non believers which are people who will listen to anything but the truth. We have to stay encouraged and keep teaching the Word of God in all situations. We have to do this in season and out of season. We have to be patient and careful and keep our minds on the work of God. We should always be about our Father's business. (Second) When Paul said I have finished the course, That meant he finished his assignments that were given to him by God. We have to stay grounded and be obedient to God's will and commands, we have to stay faithful and true and we will win. (Lastly) Paul said I have kept the faith, meaning we have to believe that God is the one and only true God, and that He is God alone.

Father, We thank you for wisdom, knowledge, and understanding. We will continue to give you all the glory and have nothing but faith in you and your word. In Jesus name...

Amen

Day 14

WE HAVE TO FORGIVE

Not rendering evil for evil, or railing for railing: but contrariwise blessing; knowing that ye are thereunto called, that ye should inherit a blessing.

--1 Peter 3:9

Don't block your blessings by holding offense in your heart. Repent to God, apologize, forgive, and move on. When we hold grudges or go tic for tac with someone we are taking God's work out of His hands. Vengeance is mine saith the Lord. When someone is being evil or saying bad things to us we have to pray for them, we have to forgive them and ask God to forgive them. We can not be bound by holding unforgiveness or malice in our hearts. God will work it.

Father, I ask that you fill us with your Spirit, we bind the spirit of offense right now in the name of Jesus, we ask that you cleanse our hearts and minds, we decree and declare that we are free from any evil that's behind these feelings. We will not be tormented, Lord your word says that there is no rest for the wicked so offense you must go right now.

In Jesus name...

Amen

Day 15

A LOVING SERVANT

Whatever you do, work at it with all your heart, as working for the Lord, not for human masters.

--Colossians 3:23

As christians we are servants of the Lord, when we serve or provide a service we need to serve like we are serving God himself. We will be rewarded by God not by man who we are only here to serve for a little bit of time. As christians we should always be excited when it's time to serve God, our character and attitude to serve will make a huge difference in and out of our ministries. All of our service should only be for Him, No matter who you are or where you are in life if you are called to do God's work do it gracefully because God is the only judge and man cannot judge us. We have a master and our master is in heaven and not on earth. This scripture is personal to me because my Apostle Owen E. Ford jr. named the ministry I'm apart of Loving Servants and that we are, we completely submit ourselves to God, Everyone that comes through our doors get greeted with a warm hug and smile and they remember it, In closing always remember it's ok to cater to someone it's not about pleasing man but pleasing God and you just don't know what someone is going through you could be the light that makes someone's light shine.

Father, we just want to thank you, we want to give you praise, honor, and glory. Lord keep our hearts free. Make your word clear to us and let it show through us. Lord let us never separate from you, but always be guided by you. We will forever serve you .
In Jesus name...
Amen

Day 16

BE OBEDIENT

Do not merely listen to the word, and so deceive yourselves. Do what it says.

--James 1:22

A lot of us don't like to follow rules or some just simply want to do what they want to do, it doesn't work that way when you believe in Christ. James is telling us that if we believe and trust God we have to adhere to and follow the word just as it is, we can't just read the word we must live it. We have to ask God to make our crooked paths straight and go where God is leading us. We talk and blurt out scriptures to others, but are we really taking the time to hear and understand what God is teaching us? The bible is the map and we have to follow the journey.

Father, we ask that we always be led by you and follow your guidance and be obedient to you at all times. Lord we ask for your direction so that we will always be with you.
In Jesus name… Amen.

Day 17

THE FAVOR OF GOD

Surely, Lord, you bless the righteous; you surround them with your favor as with a shield.

--Psalms 5:12

When we obey God and do right by Him and others, He will bless you. Blessings will come big and small, some will receive supernatural or divine blessings. Things will happen at a blank of an eye and you will be amazed. There are many testimonies of supernatural favor for example, you've been praying and fasting or you've been sowing and asking God for a miracle and miraculously debt is demolished, a loved one is healed from a disease with no cure, displaced families are back together, you get approved for a house without the credit or income to get it, and the list can go on and on about God's favor. We also need to pray for others as we pray for ourselves. God loves when we are not selfish wanting all of his glory for ourselves. As long as we believe and have faith and trust in him God will shield us with his favor.

Father, we pray that you continue to cover us with your shield of favor. We desire to be righteous and give you all the praise for the favor that you bestow upon us.

In Jesus name...

Amen

Day 18

GOOD AND EVIL

You intended to harm me, but God intended it for good to accomplish what is now being done, the saving of many lives.

--Genesis 50:20

As believers we have to believe that there is good in evil. God will always conquer evil, we will have many trials and tribulations. Unfortunately evil is one of them. God himself can cause many things to happen in our lives in the form of hurt, harm, and danger to get our attention. Things will happen to us and it will come from people we love, people we don't know, self hurt and harm or from God. We have to go through these things, to gain wisdom. God wants us to have wisdom, knowledge, and understanding. Wisdom to know what to do when the time comes, knowledge of what to do and how to fight, and understanding of why God will allow these things to happen. Once the lesson is complete then we will be able to give a powerful testimony of how we overcame evil for good, and that will allow us to save someone else.

Father, we know that trials may come but we will stay strong. Lord you didn't go through life easily so we know that our lives won't be easy. We will not be overcome with evil but we will overcome evil.

In Jesus name...

Amen

Day 19

LET YOUR LIGHT SHINE

When Jesus spoke again to the people, he said, "I am the light of the world. Whoever follows me will never walk in darkness, but will have the light of life".

--John 8:12

John wrote seven I Am declarations of Jesus, this is the second one. You will only find this in the Gospel of John. When God said that He is the light of the world that means that He is the only light. No believer that walks in God's light will walk in darkness. If we commit sins we have to repent and after repenting we can't keep committing the same sins. If we don't follow the light of God our light will go dim and the only person that can dim our light is us. God's light exposes evil and people that are evil don't like light, that's why they try to go after people that shine. God gave us all a piece of His light, let's continue being a reflection of him and shine wherever we are.

Father, we thank you for giving us a piece of your light. We pray that we continue to shine no matter the circumstance because darkness has no place for us. We pray that the people of darkness repent so that they begin to follow you and their light will begin to shine and it will never go dim.

In Jesus name...

Amen

Day 20

HE HAS OUR BACK

Lord, be gracious to us; we long for you. Be our strength every morning, our salvation in times of distress.

--Isaiah 33:2

As soon as we wake in the morning we should pray or talk to God before we do anything else. We should ask God for strength in order to get through the day. We need to commit our day to God by focusing on Him as soon as we get up. Often times we turn on the television, pick up the phone to check messages or missed calls, we log onto social media and so forth we get so distracted, but if you wake up Pray, meditate, or lay still and wait to hear from the lord your day will turn out so much better. He will give us the strength that we need until morning comes again.

Father, we thank you in advance for all that you do for us, we thank you for breathing the breath of life in us. We thank you for always protecting us and we thank you for giving us the strength to get through today and everyday.

In Jesus name...

Amen

Day 21

NO WEAPON FORMED WILL PROSPER

No weapon formed against you shall prosper, and every tongue that rises against you in judgement you shall condemn. This is the heritage of the servants of the Lord, and their righteousness is from me, says the Lord.

--Isaiah 54:17

People will lie to you, accuse you of untrue things and gossip about you, but when you are walking with the Lord it's nothing they can really do. No weapon, no person, nothing can form against you it will not prosper. You have to condemn them with the truth and that will set you free. God will protect you at all times. God will give you the victory in troubled times. The god that we serve will never leave you or forsake you. God's righteousness will always prevail when you are walking with Him, you will have peace just by knowing we have a God that's always ready to protect us. He will make sure our truth is known and most times we don't have to say or do anything because God had it worked out already.

Father, I thank you so much for your covering, for clearing my ear gates so that I could hear only your voice as I was writing this devotional, Father I pray that these scriptures touch the hearts and minds of everyone who reads it. Father I just thank you for your favor for your grace for your mercy. This is my season and I promise I will lay at your feet and continue to give you praise, honor, and glory. Father i put you first in all that I do and I just thank you for giving me the courage and strength to start and finish this journey. You word says that all that I set my hands to do will prosper and I receive that in the name of Jesus, No weapon formed against me will prosper, it won't work.

In Jesus name...

Amen

www.ingramcontent.com/pod-product-compliance
Lightning Source LLC
Chambersburg PA
CBHW070949180426
43194CB00041B/1995